See additional verses inside.

CUMBAYAH

FLOYD COOPER

MORROW JUNIOR BOOKS
NEW YORK

FOR ANDREA

Special thanks to Tom Miller for researching the origins of the song.
Oil wash on illustration board was used for the full-color illustrations. The text type is 22-point Schneidler.

Published by Morrow Junior Books
a division of William Morrow and Company, Inc.
1350 Avenue of the Americas, New York, NY 10019
www.williammorrow.com

Printed in the United States of America.

1 2 3 4 5 6 7 8 9 10

Library of Congress Cataloging-in-Publication Data
Cooper, Floyd.
Cumbayah/Floyd Cooper.
p. cm.
Summary: An illustrated version of the popular folk song. Printed music on endpapers.
ISBN 0-688-13543-9 (trade)—ISBN 0-688-13544-7 (library)
1. Folk songs, English—United States—Texts. [1. Folk songs—United States.]
I. Title.   PZ8.3.C783Cu 1998   782.42—dc21   [E]   96-44323   CIP AC

A NOTE ABOUT THIS BOOK

You've probably heard the song "Cumbayah" many different times in your life—at camp, in church, in music class, or maybe even in your mother's lap when you were a baby. But have you ever wondered what "Cumbayah" really means?

"Cumbayah" (also known as "Kum Ba Yah" and "Kumbaya") means "come by here" in the Gullah dialect. The Gullah people live on the Sea Islands, which are off the coast of Georgia, South Carolina, and Florida. Over the years the Gullah have maintained an extraordinary connection to African culture, evident in their language, music, and traditions.

Though the sources of this beloved folk song have been the subject of much debate, it's agreed by most that the song actually originated in the United States rather than in Africa. It may have been a hymn sung by nineteenth-century Gullah who had converted to Christianity, or it may have evolved among their twentieth-century descendants. It wasn't until the mid-1920s that the earliest field recordings of the song were made, and its first publication was in 1931. Soon after, a gospel chorus titled "Come by Here" was written by Marvin Frey and then used by a missionary couple as they worked in Angola. This was most likely the song's first appearance in an African country.

Some twenty years later, the song made a comeback as a spiritual during the civil rights movement and folk-song revival of the 1950s and 1960s. Since then, many adaptations and versions have been printed and sung throughout the nation. It has endured as an American folk-song standard.

In this book, the song's meaning reaches beyond its African-American roots. The words and my pictures are reminders of what all of us share—for no matter who or where we are, there are moments in everyone's lives when we need someone to "come by here."

With the simple melody, the song allows for easy participation. Try creating verses of your own that are meaningful to you, as I have done in this book.

—Floyd Cooper

Cumbayah, my Lord, cumbayah,
Cumbayah, my Lord, cumbayah,
Cumbayah, my Lord, cumbayah,
Oh, Lord, cumbayah.

Someone's singing, Lord, cumbayah,
Someone's singing, Lord, cumbayah,
Someone's singing, Lord, cumbayah,
Oh, Lord, cumbayah.

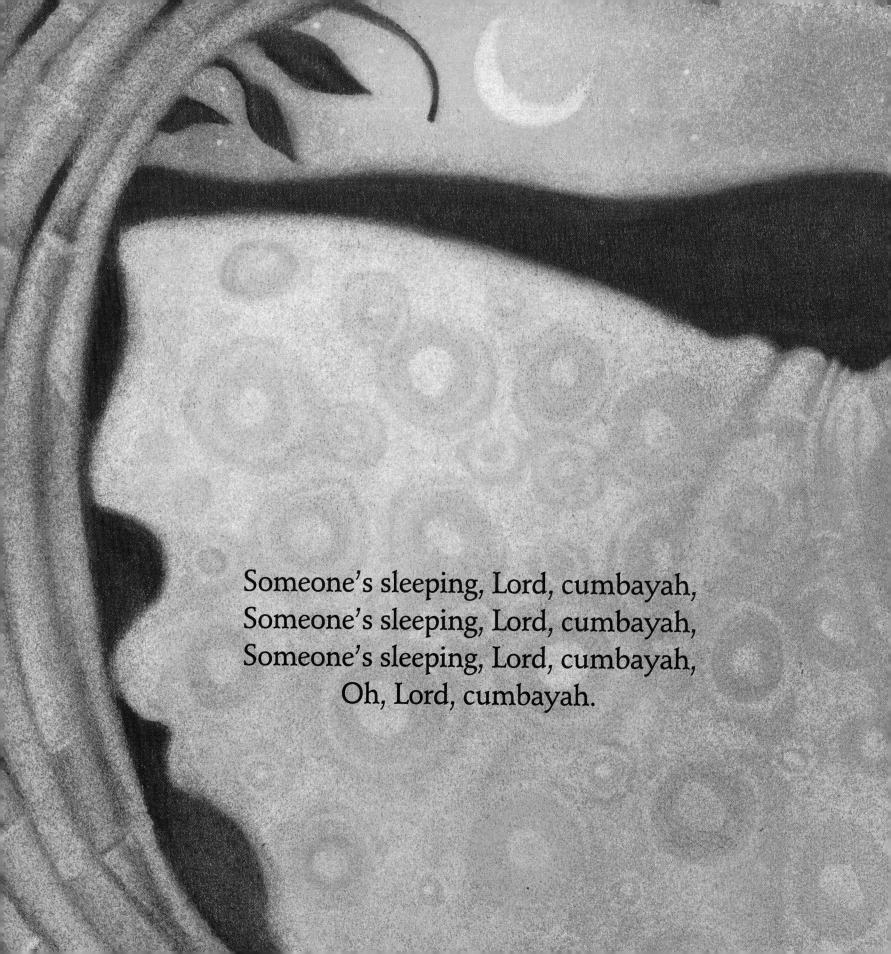

Someone's sleeping, Lord, cumbayah,
Someone's sleeping, Lord, cumbayah,
Someone's sleeping, Lord, cumbayah,
Oh, Lord, cumbayah.

Someone's working, Lord, cumbayah,
Someone's working, Lord, cumbayah,
Someone's working, Lord, cumbayah,
Oh, Lord, cumbayah.

Someone's crying, Lord, cumbayah,
Someone's crying, Lord, cumbayah,
Someone's crying, Lord, cumbayah,
Oh, Lord, cumbayah.

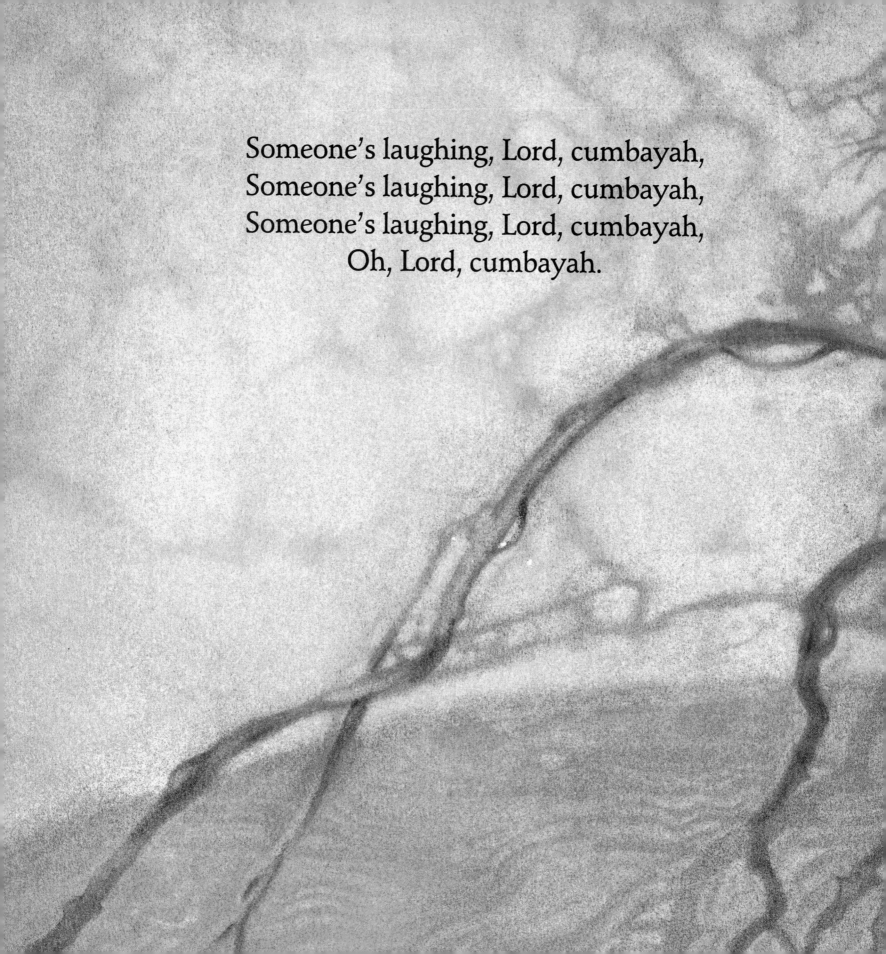

Someone's laughing, Lord, cumbayah,
Someone's laughing, Lord, cumbayah,
Someone's laughing, Lord, cumbayah,
Oh, Lord, cumbayah.

Someone's hurting, Lord, cumbayah,
Someone's hurting, Lord, cumbayah,
Someone's hurting, Lord, cumbayah,
Oh, Lord, cumbayah.

Someone's dancing, Lord, cumbayah,
Someone's dancing, Lord, cumbayah,
Someone's dancing, Lord, cumbayah,
Oh, Lord, cumbayah.

Someone needs You, Lord, cumbayah,
Someone needs You, Lord, cumbayah,
Someone needs You, Lord, cumbayah,
Oh, Lord, cumbayah.

Someone's praising You, cumbayah,
Someone's praising You, cumbayah,
Someone's praising You, cumbayah,

Oh,
Lord,
cumbayah.

CUMBAYAH

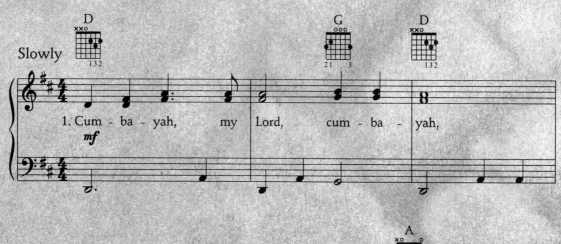